LEMONS

HARLAXTON
PUBLISHING

BRIDGET JONES

Harlaxton Publishing Limited
2 Avenue Road
Grantham
Lincolnshire NG31 6TA United Kingdom
A Member of the Weldon International Group of Companies.

First published in 1993.

© 1993	Copyright Harlaxton Publishing Limited
© 1993	Copyright design Harlaxton Publishing Limited
Publisher:	Robin Burgess
Design & Coordination:	Rachel Rush
Cover Photography:	Chris Allen, Forum Advertising Limited
Food Photography:	James Duncan
Stylist:	Madelaine Brehaut
Home Economist:	Joanna Farrow
Illustrator:	Valerie Littlewood
Editor:	Alison Leach
Typesetting:	John Macauley, Seller's, Grantham, UK
Colour separation:	GA Graphics, Stamford UK
Printing:	Imago, Singapore

British Library Cataloguing-in-Publication data.
A catalogue record for this book is available from the British Library.

Title:	Lemons
ISBN:	1-85837-106-6

CONTENTS

 # INTRODUCTION

With the wide range of exotic produce that is now available from all over the world, the humble lemon is taken for granted, yet its full flavour, acidic juice and zesty rind set it apart as one of the most versatile fruits. When doing some research on lemons, I found that there are different theories about the origins of the fruit, some sources suggesting that it probably originated in India and others suggesting that it was first cultivated in Japan or China. Lemons were introduced to Europe by the Moors who planted trees in Spain and who can probably also be credited for introducing them to Sicily. Whatever the true history, lemons are now widely cultivated in warmer climates within a band of about 40° north or south of the equator; the principal growing areas include Italy, Spain and California.

Unlike other varieties of citrus fruit, no distinction is made by retailers between the types of lemons available. This is largely because many of them have very similar qualities. Unwaxed fruit is, however, identified. The majority of lemons are coated with a harmless wax to reduce moisture loss by evaporation.

Some lemons have very fine skin and are slightly more rounded in shape and smaller. They usually have a thinner layer of pith under the rind and are therefore more attractive when cut for garnishes or decorations. The rougher, larger and more elongated fruit tends to have a thicker layer of pith and, often, more pips (seeds). Sometimes these lemons seem to yield slightly less juice but this is something I have noticed in use rather than by direct comparison.

Rarely is the entire fruit used in cooking – there are exceptions such as an extremely spicy pickle made with chunks of lemon or a custard tart topped with thinly sliced lemons – the rind is usually grated or pared (very thinly peeled) off the fruit and the juice is squeezed out separately. The pith is not generally used as is it has a bitter taste which can dominate a dish – so do not be tempted to peel a lemon thickly instead of paring the rind.

However, both the pith and pips are rich sources of pectin which is an essential ingredient in making set preserves, such as jams, marmalades and jellies. Pectin is a type of binding ingredient found in plant cells and it is extracted by boiling. The pith and pips are then discarded and sugar is added. When the proportion of sugar is correctly balanced with the pectin by fast boiling to reduce the volume of liquid, the mixture will set on cooling. Acid is the only other ingredient which is essential for achieving a good set and, of course, lemons provide plenty of acid in their juice. The acidic juice is also valued as a dressing for rich or oily foods.

Away from the kitchen, lemons lend their fresh scent to a variety of household products and the fruit itself may be used to make pomanders. On the beauty front, the astringent and delicate bleaching qualities of lemon juice may be used to create home-made potions and lotions to improve the complexion.

 ## COOK'S NOTES

Standard spoon and cup measurements are used in all recipes. All spoon and cup measurements are level.

1 tablespoon = 15 ml spoon

1 teaspoon   = 5 ml spoon

As the imperial/metric/US equivalents are not exact, follow only one system of measurement.

Ovens should be preheated to the specified temperature.

Fresh herbs are used unless otherwise stated. If they are unavailable, use half the quantity of dried herbs.

Use freshly ground black pepper unless white is indicated. Salt and pepper is added according to your individual taste.

Use only natural vanilla essence (extract) and not synthetic vanilla flavouring.

ABOVE: Lemons arranged in a glass dish with bay leaves and a ribbon bow (p.12)

DISCOVERING LEMONS

LEMON GARNISHES & DECORATIONS

The lemon, must be one of the most widely used savoury garnishes. Avoid adding a slim slice of lemon simply because no other garnish is available but do use this refreshing fruit to improve the appearance of appropriate dishes.

WEDGES	These should be served for their juice, not for their appearance alone. Arrange them on grilled or fried fish and seafood, poultry and lamb. The juice is squeezed over the food before it is eaten.
SLICES	Large lemons with a thick layer of pith do not produce attractive slices. So look for small, slightly rounded fruit with comparatively fine-textured skin.
COG-WHEEL EDGES	Use a parer to cut off fine but thick strips of lemon rind along the length of the fruit before slicing.
LEMON TWISTS	Cut a fairly thin slice of fruit, then make a cut in as far as the centre of the fruit. Twist the cut edges of the slit in opposite directions so that the slice can stand.
LEMON ROSES	Use a small, very sharp knife to cut the rind off the fruit in a long thin strip which will curl around slightly. Do not cut any pith with the rind. Roll the rind into a rose shape.
PARED LEMON STRIPS	Pare the rind off as above, then cut it into very fine strips. Cook these in boiling water for 15 minutes, drain and use as a garnish or decoration on savoury or sweet dishes.
VANDYKE CUT	Use a sharp, pointed knife to cut around the middle of a lemon, cutting in as far as the centre of the fruit and alternating the angle of each cut. When you have cut all around the fruit, pull the two halves apart.
LEMON CUT-OUTS	Pare the rind from the fruit and cook it in boiling water for 10 minutes, then drain well. Use a small pointed knife to cut diamond or leaf shapes. Tiny aspic cutters may be used to stamp out flowers and other shapes.
LEMON SHELL	Cut the top off a lemon and scoop out the fruit. Trim the end of the shell so that it stands steadily. Fill with fish pâté or sorbet (and freeze again). Halved lemon shells may be filled with salad garnish, herb sprigs or petits pois for adding to fish platters.

BELOW: Decorative lemon garnishes

 # LEMON DRINKS

Lemons play a versatile role in both alcoholic and non-alcoholic beverages, from flavouring soothing cold cures to creating zesty summer coolers. Thin slices of lemon may be added to weak tea instead of milk, particularly China tea, delicate Earl Grey or smoky lapsang souchong.

CITRUS ZINGER

Pare the rind of 1 lemon in short strips, working around the fruit so that they curl slightly. Place these in a jug with the juice of the lemon, about 12 thin cucumber slices and 125 ml/4 fl oz/ ½ cup orange liqueur (for example, Curaçao or Cointreau). Top up with sparkling dry white wine and add plenty of ice cubes. Stir well and serve. For a less potent drink, use half a bottle of still or semi-sparkling white wine and an equal quantity of sparkling mineral water.

HOT LEMON & HONEY

A soothing drink for sore throats. Pare the rind from 1 lemon and squeeze its juice into a heatproof glass or mug. Add 1 tablespoon honey and the lemon rind, top up with boiling water and leave to stand for 5 minutes before drinking.

ICED LEMON MINT TEA

Make some weak tea, preferably China, Darjeeling or Earl Grey. Strain the brewed tea into a jug. Add the pared rind of 1 lemon, ½ lemon cut into thin slices and 4 small mint sprigs. Cover and leave until cold. Add sugar to taste and ice cubes to the tea before serving.

LEMON BARLEY WATER

Bring 30 g/1 oz/3 tablespoons pearl barley to the boil in a saucepan of water. Drain the barley, then return it to the pan. Add the pared rind from 2 lemons and 1.15 litres/2 pints/ 5 cups cold water. Bring to the boil, reduce the heat, cover and simmer for 30 minutes. Leave to cool. Strain and add the juice of 2 lemons with sugar to taste. Serve chilled.

 ## LEMON ROSEMARY TEA

Pare the rind from 1 lemon and place it in a heated small tea pot with a 5 cm/2 inch sprig of rosemary. Add 1 teaspoon Darjeeling tea and top up with fresh boiling water. Leave to brew for 8 minutes, then strain into two cups. Sweeten to taste and serve with lemon slices and rosemary sprigs.

LEMON YOGHURT REFRESHER

A good early-morning drink! In a tall glass, mix the grated rind and juice from $\frac{1}{2}$ lemon with 125 ml/4 fl oz/ $\frac{1}{2}$ cup plain yoghurt. Add 1-2 teaspoons clear honey and stir well. Top up with sparkling mineral water, adding slightly less than the volume of lemon yoghurt. Drink at once.

LEMON WHISKY TODDY

An extra-warming version of the above, this will soothe away those tedious symptoms of an approaching cold. Add whisky to the lemon and honey to fill about a third of the glass and top up with boiling water.

QUICK SPARKLING LEMONADE

Grate the rind and juice from 3 lemons and bring to the boil with 125 g/4 oz/ $\frac{1}{2}$ cup granulated sugar and 125 ml/4 fl oz/ $\frac{1}{2}$ cup water. Remove from the heat and add a few ice cubes to cool the syrup quickly. Pour it into a jug and top up with a well-chilled bottle of sparkling mineral water.

STILL LEMONADE

Pare the rind and squeeze the juice from 3 large lemons. Place the rind and juice in a saucepan and add 125 g/4 oz/ $\frac{1}{2}$ cup granulated sugar. Stir in 1.15 litres/2 pints/5 cups water. Bring to the boil, reduce the heat and cover the pan. Simmer gently for 30 minutes, then cool. Strain the lemonade into a jug and taste for sweetness, stirring in a little extra sugar if liked. Chill well. Float thin lemon slices in the drink when serving.

NEXT PAGE: LEFT TO RIGHT: Quick Sparkling Lemonade; Hot Lemon and Honey; Lemon Rosemary Tea

FRESHENERS & DECORATIONS

Here are a few ideas which may inspire you to experiment with non-culinary uses for citrus fruit.

A BOWL OF LEMONS & BAY LEAVES

Instead of having the usual floral table centrepiece, build a pyramid of perfect lemons in a wide, shallow dish. Use waxed lemons which do not dry out in a warm room as quickly as unwaxed ones. Pile them in the dish (a brass one looks particularly good) and arrange large bay leaves and small sprigs of fresh bay between the fruit.

LEMON & ROSEMARY POMANDERS

These impart an excellent fresh scent. Although pomanders were originally intended as cupboard (closet) fresheners to deter moths from invading the contents, in our modern homes they may be heaped high in a dish to give their aroma to the room. I hang them on the coat-stand in our hall and their scent is particularly noticeable when walking downstairs.

Stick cloves all over a large lemon, working around the fruit in neat rows. When half the lemon is studded with cloves, stick a row of short but sturdy rosemary sprigs around the middle of the fruit. Then finish studding the rest of the lemon with cloves. Tie a length of fine baby ribbon around the fruit, securing it with a knot on the top. Tie another length, again knotting it at the top but on the opposite side of the fruit. Tie the ribbon ends into loops for hanging the pomander. If you use fine ribbon, it will lie neatly and securely between the cloves.

NIGHT-LIGHT CUPS

Halve and scoop out the lemon as above. Remove the foil from a night-light and place it in one of the shells. Individual cups may be placed on saucers and surrounded with small flowers or foliage. Groups of cups are more effective – arrange at least three shells together with a small flower, foliage or ribbon loops in between. A large shallow bowl may be filled with night-light cups, with decorative shells, pebbles, foliage and flowers added. Alternatively, settle the night-light cups in a large shallow dish containing glass marbles or beads.

Pomander Pot-Pourri Cups

Cut a large lemon in half and scoop out all the flesh, leaving just the shell of pith and rind. Trim the bases of each half shell, if necessary, so that they stand steadily. Stud them with cloves, fill with pot-pourri and stand on decorative saucers.

Lemon Candle Holders

A good way of using lemon shells when the juice has been squeezed out and ideal for small candles, measuring about 10 cm/4 inches high and 12 mm/ ¹⁄₂ inch diameter.

Cut a lemon in half, squeeze out the juice, and scrape out all the membranes, leaving a neat pith and rind shell. Stand the shell cut-side down and check that it makes an even dome; if not, trim one side of the cut edge very slightly so that it stands evenly. Use a sharp, pointed knife to cut out the stalk end, making a hole slightly smaller than the diameter of the candle.

Place one or two flowers and leaves in the hole before pushing in the candle, then tie a bow of narrow ribbon around the base of the candle. Place on a saucer or suitable shallow dish.

Use yellow or green candles, daisies or miniature narcissi and small, feathery leaves for an Easter table decoration. Red candles, ivy and red ribbon are ideal for Christmas or, match the candles and flowers to your table colour scheme.

ABOVE: A selection of attractive gifts:
Lemon Candle Holders; Lemon and Rosemary Pomanders; Lemon Barley Water (p.8) with beauty preparations

Most people's skin seems to benefit from a change of treatment but abandoning half-used products for a new range of cosmetics can be extremely expensive. Instead, why not give your complexion a break with these simple potions? I often feel that it is not what I put on my face that does good so much as the fact that I have bothered to pay it some much-needed attention. Even if your complexion is not restored to the full-bloom of youth, you will feel a whole lot better for lying down and relaxing — make yourself some lemon and rosemary tea, and play some gentle background music.

FRAGRANT BATH SOAP

Pare and roughly chop the rind and squeeze the juice from 2 lemons. Place in a small saucepan and pour in 125 ml/4 fl oz/ ^{1}⁄2 cup water. Bring to the boil, reduce the heat and cover the pan. Simmer for 15 minutes and then boil, uncovered, for 2 minutes. Strain the liquid and leave to cool. Stir the lemon liquid, about 4 drops of peppermint essence and 1 tablespoon sweet almond oil into 125 ml/4 fl oz/ ^{1}⁄2 cup unperfumed liquid soap. Add some to the bath, pouring it under the running hot water.

LEMON HAIR RINSE

Place the juice of 1 lemon in a jug and top it up to about 600 ml/1 pint /2^1⁄2 cups with hand-hot water. Use this as a final rinse once you have washed away all the shampoo. Use very infrequently on two or three successive occasions to help remove any build-up of conditioner.

 ## LEMON FRESHENER

Mix the strained juice of 1 lemon with an equal quantity of rosewater. Keep in the refrigerator or a cool place and dab over the skin with cotton wool pads.

OATMEAL FACE PACK

Lightly whisk 1 egg white with the juice of ½ lemon and 1 teaspoon sweet almond oil. Stir in enough medium or fine oatmeal to make a paste. Spread this evenly over your face and leave for 20-30 minutes. Rinse off with lukewarm water.

TONING MASK

Lightly whisk 1 egg white with the juice of 1 lemon. Stir in enough cornflour (cornstarch) to make a thin paste. Brush this on with a clean, soft make-up brush. Allow to dry for a few minutes, then brush on another layer. Leave for 20 minutes before rinsing off.

ABOVE: Oatmeal Face Pack; Lemon Freshener

SALADS & STARTERS

Open a meal on a zesty note or make an aromatic salad to complement a plain main dish. The recipes in this section are also ideal for a light summer lunch or simple evening meal.

Couscous Salad

For the first course of a meal, serve this zesty salad with crusty bread to mop the juices. It is also delicious with plain grilled lamb or fish.

SERVES 4	150 g/5 oz /1 cup	couscous
	300 ml/ $^1/_2$ pint /1$^1/_4$ cups	boiling water
	6	spring onions (scallions), chopped
	2	celery sticks, diced
	1	red pepper, seeded and diced
	4 tablespoons	chopped parsley
		Grated rind and juice of 1 lemon
	1	garlic clove, crushed
		Salt and pepper
	1 teaspoon	caster (superfine) sugar
	4 tablespoons	olive oil

Place the couscous in a bowl and pour in the boiling water. Cover and leave to stand for 30 minutes, by which time the grains will be swollen and all the water will be absorbed.

Fork the spring onions, celery, red pepper and parsley into the couscous. Whisk the lemon rind and juice, garlic, seasoning and sugar together in a small basin until the sugar has dissolved. Then whisk in the oil gradually. Pour this dressing over the salad, mix lightly and leave to stand, covered, for at least 30 minutes before serving.

PRAWNS & OYSTER MUSHROOMS

	Pared rind of 1 lemon
4 teaspoons	chopped tarragon
4	spring onions (scallions), chopped
	Salt and pepper
450 g/1 lb	peeled cooked prawns (shrimp), thawed and drained if frozen
275 g/10 oz	oyster mushrooms, halved or quartered if large
2 tablespoons	olive oil
30 g/1 oz /2 tablespoons	butter

Cut the strips of lemon rind across into fine shreds. Place in a small saucepan with water to cover. Bring to the boil, reduce the heat and simmer for 5 minutes. Drain the lemon rind and place it in a bowl. Add the tarragon, spring onions, plenty of seasoning and the prawns. Mix the ingredients well and then lightly toss in the mushrooms. Cover and set aside for 30-60 minutes.

Heat the oil and butter in a large frying pan (skillet). Tip the mixture into the pan, scraping out the bowl well. Sauté the mixture over high heat for about 5 minutes, turning the ingredients all the time until thoroughly hot. Serve at once.

ABOVE: TOP: Couscous Salad - BOTTOM: Lemon Prawns with Oyster Mushrooms

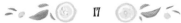

 **BROWN BREAD SALAD**

Richly flavoured with anchovies, lemon and basil,
this peasant-style salad is excellent for lunch and
an interesting option for a dinner-party first course.

SERVES 4

1	*lemon*
50 g/2 oz	*can anchovies, chopped*
1	*garlic clove, chopped*
8	*black olives, stoned (pitted) and chopped*
1 tablespoon	*chopped capers*
4	*spring onions (scallions), chopped*
3 tablespoons	*good olive oil*
	Salt and pepper
	Freshly grated nutmeg
6	*medium slices wholemeal (wholewheat) bread*
8	*large basil leaves*
	Lemon wedges to serve
About 8	*endive (chicory) leaves, shredded (optional)*

Use a parer or small knife to cut fine strips of rind off the lemon, working around the fruit in a circular pattern. Place the rind in a saucepan with water to cover and bring to the boil, reduce the heat and simmer for 5 minutes.

Meanwhile, chop the anchovies and mix them with the oil from the can. Drain and chop the lemon rind and add it to the anchovies with the garlic, olives, capers and spring onions. Stir in the olive oil, seasoning and a little nutmeg.

Place the bread under the grill (broiler) or in a toaster and toast until dry but not browned on both sides. Cut the bread into small dice and place in a bowl. Pour the anchovy mixture over and toss the salad well immediately so that all the bread is coated. Use scissors to shred the basil over the salad. Cover and leave to marinate for 1 hour.

Toss the salad again before serving with lemon wedges so that their juice may be squeezed over the bread to taste. The salad may be piled on a base of shredded endive leaves.

OPPOSITE: TOP: Brown Bread Salad - BOTTOM: Coconut Salad (p.20)

Coconut Salad

SERVES 4

This vaguely oriental salad really zips the tastebuds to life! It is quick and easy to prepare, and ideal for serving with plain steamed or grilled (broiled) poultry or fish. Serve it as a first course for an oriental menu or as a type of relish.

Grate 125 g/4 oz/1 cup fresh coconut flesh (about ½ coconut) coarsely. Mix it with 1 teaspoon caster (superfine) sugar, grated rind of 1 lemon, juice of ½ lemon, 1 crushed garlic clove, 4 chopped spring onions (scallions), 1 seeded and chopped green chilli, 2 tablespoons shredded mint and 1 teaspoon light soy sauce. Toss the ingredients until the sugar has dissolved. Then toss in ¼ teaspoon sesame oil and 1 tablespoon sunflower oil – delicious!

Chicken Soup

SERVES 4

	Knob of butter
1	*chicken quarter*
1	*garlic clove, crushed*
1	*bay leaf*
1	*thyme sprig*
2	*parsley sprigs*
1	*onion, chopped*
1	*celery stick, diced*
1	*carrot, diced*
1	*potato, diced*
	Pared rind and juice of 1 lemon
1.15 litres/2 pints/5 cups	*chicken stock*
	Salt and pepper
200 ml/7 fl oz/¾ cup	*single (light) cream*
	croûtons, made with 2 slices bread
2 tablespoons	*chopped parsley*
6	*black olives, stoned (pitted) and chopped*

Melt the butter in a large saucepan. Add the chicken quarter and brown it all over. Arrange the garlic, herbs, vegetables and lemon rind in the pan. Cover and cook gently for 15 minutes.

Pour in the stock and bring to the boil. Reduce the heat, cover and simmer for 45 minutes. Lift the chicken from the stock. Discard the skin and dice the meat. Discard the herbs and purée the soup in a blender or by rubbing it through a sieve (strainer). Reheat the soup, stir in the chicken, lemon juice and seasoning. Reduce the heat to a minimum, stir in the cream and heat briefly. Do not allow the soup to simmer or the cream will curdle.

Mix the croûtons, parsley and chopped olives. Sprinkle this mixture over portions of the soup before serving. Offer the remaining croûton mixture separately.

 # MAIN DISHES

This selection of recipes is intended to inspire you to experiment with lemon in a broad variety of savoury cooking. Remember that lemon can be used as a dominant flavouring or it can be the elusive ingredient which makes the dish: in both cases its role is equally valuable.

MONKFISH WITH ASPARAGUS

SERVES 4

60 g/2 oz/ ^{1}⁄$_4$ cup	butter
675 g/1^1⁄$_2$ lb	monkfish (goosefish) fillet
	Pared rind of 1 lemon, finely shredded
1	young carrot, cut into fine strips
1	small leek, thinly sliced
	Salt and pepper
1	bay leaf
450 g/1 lb	asparagus
	Lemon wedges to serve

Grease an ovenproof dish with a little of the butter. Lay the monkfish in the dish. Blanch the lemon, carrot and leek together in boiling water for 2 minutes. Drain and sprinkle over the fish. Top with seasoning, the bay leaf and half the remaining butter, cover the dish tightly and bake at 190°C/375°F/gas 5 for 30 minutes.

Trim off any woody ends from the asparagus and cook the spears in boiling salted water for 4-5 minutes, until just tender. Arrange on the monkfish with the remaining butter. Cover the dish tightly and cook in the oven for 5 minutes. Serve the monkfish, sliced into medallions with the vegetables, cooking juices and lemon wedges.

 **LAMB WITH TOMATO MARINADE**

SERVES 4

4	lamb steaks
	Salt and pepper
	Pared rind of 1 lemon, chopped
4	sun-dried tomatoes, chopped
2	rosemary sprigs
4 tablespoons	olive oil
250 ml/8 fl oz/1 cup	red wine
30 g/1 oz/¼ cup	lightly salted pistachio nuts, shelled and chopped
4	basil leaves

Place the lamb steaks in a single layer in a dish. Sprinkle with seasoning, then lemon rind, tomatoes and rosemary on top. Pour the oil and wine over, cover and chill overnight or for up to 48 hours, depending on the freshness of the lamb.

Drain the lamb, scraping all the marinade from the steaks. Pour the marinade into a saucepan and bring to the boil. Reduce the heat, cover and simmer gently for 20 minutes. Cook the lamb steaks under a hot grill (broiler), allowing 4-6 minutes on each side, depending on how you like the lamb cooked and the thickness of the steaks.

To finish the sauce, boil it hard for 2 minutes and taste for seasoning. Discard the herbs and spoon the sauce on warmed serving plates. Lay the steaks on top of the sauce. Sprinkle each steak with basil and pistachio nuts. Serve at once.

Goujons are slim strips of food coated with breadcrumbs. Traditionally, they are deep-fried but this
simple method works well.

SERVES 4

Beat 1 egg with 1 tablespoon oil. Mix the grated rind of 1 lemon, 150 g/5 oz/1^{1}₄ cups dried white breadcrumbs and 1
teaspoon dried thyme with seasoning. Cut 450 g/1 lb skinned turkey breast fillet into slim strips.

Place a little flour in a bowl. Coat each strip of turkey with flour, the beaten egg and the breadcrumb mixture. Press
the breadcrumbs on well and place the coated strips on a greased baking sheet. Bake the goujons at 200°C/400°F/
gas 6 for about 25 minutes, until the coating is browned and the turkey cooked through. Serve at once, with wedges of
lemon, so that the juice may be squeezed over, and salad.

ABOVE: Baked Turkey Goujons with Lemon Mayonnaise (p.43)

GOLDEN FISH

Mustard and turmeric combine with lemon to
create a piquant seasoning for this simple fish dish.
Serve it on rice or with pasta tossed with butter.

SERVES 4

675 g/1¹₂ lb	*thick white fish fillet, such as hoki, cod or haddock, skinned and cut in chunks*
1 tablespoon	*plain (all-purpose) flour*
	Salt and pepper
¹₂ teaspoon	*turmeric*
1 teaspoon	*dry mustard*
	Grated rind of 1 lemon
30 g/1 oz/2 tablespoons	*butter*
2 tablespoons	*oil*
1	*leek, thinly sliced*
375 g/13 oz	*can sweetcorn kernels, drained*
200 ml/7 fl oz/³₄ cup	*fish stock*
125 ml/4 fl oz / ¹₂ cup	*medium sweet cider*
2 tablespoons	*chopped dill*

Mix the fish, flour, plenty of seasoning, the turmeric, mustard and lemon rind until all the pieces of fish are well coated. Heat the butter and oil in a large frying pan (skillet). Add the leek and cook, stirring, for 5 minutes.

Add the fish to the pan and cook fairly quickly, turning the chunks carefully, until lightly browned in parts but not cooked through. Stir in the sweetcorn, stock and cider. Bring to the boil, stirring carefully, and then reduce the heat. Simmer for 5 minutes, or until the fish is cooked. Taste the sauce for seasoning. Stir in the dill and serve at once.

 ## STUFFED SQUID

SERVES 4

1	large onion
90 g/3 oz/1½ cups	fresh breadcrumbs
2	garlic cloves, crushed
	Grated rind of 1 lemon
2 tablespoons	chopped parsley
	Salt and pepper
1 tablespoon	lemon juice
1 tablespoon	melted butter
12 (or 8 if large)	squid, cleaned
2 tablespoons	olive oil
1	red pepper, seeded, halved and sliced
1 teaspoon	granulated sugar
1 teaspoon	dried oregano
400 g/14 oz	can chopped tomatoes

Cut about a third off the onion and chop this finely. Slice the larger portion and set it aside. Mix together the chopped onion, breadcrumbs, garlic, lemon rind, parsley, seasoning, lemon juice and butter.

Rinse the squid sacs and dry them on paper towels. The tentacles may be cut from the head, finely chopped and mixed with the breadcrumb stuffing if liked. It is easiest to use your fingers to push the stuffing into the squid – do not overfill them as the mixture expands greatly on cooking. Secure the opening of each with a wooden cocktail stick (toothpick).

Heat the olive oil in a frying pan (skillet). Sauté the sliced onion and red pepper, then transfer to a baking dish. Brown the stuffed squid quickly on both sides but do not allow to cook for long or the stuffing will escape. Mix the sugar, oregano, tomatoes and seasoning with the onion and peppers, and lay the squid on top. Cover and bake at 180°C/350°F/gas 4 for 45 minutes. Remove the cocktail sticks before serving.

NEXT PAGE: LEFT TO RIGHT: Golden Fish; Stuffed Squid

Zesty Chicken & Potato Curry

Potatoes are an excellent ingredient for combining with spices. Here they add substance to the curry and the waxy texture of new potatoes goes extremely well with the refreshing lemon. Ghee is clarified butter; ordinary butter or oil may be substituted.

Serves 4

	Pared rind of 1 lemon
60 g/2 oz/ ¼ cup	ghee
4	boneless chicken breasts, skinned and cubed
1 tablespoon	cumin seeds
6	green cardamoms
2	onions, halved and thinly sliced
3	garlic cloves, crushed
30 g/1 oz/ ¼ cup	fresh root ginger, grated
1	bay leaf
1 teaspoon	turmeric
2 tablespoons	ground coriander
1 teaspoon	ground fenugreek
	Salt and pepper
600 ml/1 pint/2½ cups	chicken stock
	Juice of ½ lemon
450 g/1 lb	small new potatoes, halved
1 tablespoon	chopped coriander (cilantro) leaves

Shred the lemon rind finely. Melt the ghee in a saucepan. Add the chicken and lemon, then brown the breasts lightly. Stir in the cumin, cardamoms, onions, garlic, ginger and bay leaf. Cook, stirring, for 10 minutes. Stir in the turmeric, coriander, fenugreek and seasoning. Add the stock and lemon juice, and bring to the boil.

Add the potatoes, reduce the heat and cover the pan tightly. Simmer gently for 45-50 minutes, until the chicken and potatoes are tender and well flavoured, uncovering the pan for the final 15 minutes. Stir occasionally during the cooking time. Taste for seasoning before serving sprinkled with chopped coriander leaves.

 ## LAMB WITH CARAWAY & LEMON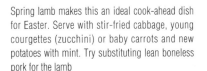

Spring lamb makes this an ideal cook-ahead dish
for Easter. Serve with stir-fried cabbage, young
courgettes (zucchini) or baby carrots and new
potatoes with mint. Try substituting lean boneless
pork for the lamb

SERVES 4

675 g/1¹⁄₂ lb	*lean boneless lamb, cubed*
1 tablespoon	*caraway seeds*
	Salt and pepper
1	*garlic clove, crushed*
	Pared rind of 2 lemons
2 tablespoons	*plain (all-purpose) flour*
2 tablespoons	*oil*
2	*onions, halved and thinly sliced*
1	*celery stick, thinly sliced*
1	*carrot, diced*
1	*bay leaf*
2	*thyme sprigs*
475 ml/16 fl oz/2 cups	*lamb or chicken stock*
	Juice of ¹⁄₂ lemon
250 ml/8 fl oz/1 cup	*single (light) cream*
2 tablespoons	*chopped parsley*
2 tablespoons	*chopped mint*

Toss the lamb with the caraway seeds, plenty of seasoning, garlic, lemon rind and flour. Heat the oil in a flameproof
casserole, add the lamb and brown the pieces all over. Stir in the onions, celery, carrot, bay leaf and thyme, and cook
for about 10 minutes, or until the vegetables are slightly softened.

Pour in the stock and add the lemon juice. Heat, stirring, until the liquid is only just boiling. Then reduce the heat,
cover the pan and simmer gently for 1 hour, or until the lamb is tender and well flavoured. Taste for seasoning before
stirring in the cream. Heat briefly without allowing the sauce to simmer. Sprinkle the mixed parsley and mint over the
lamb before serving.

 29

 **CHICKEN BALLOTINE**

SERVES 6

6	boneless chicken breasts, skinned
	Knob of butter
125 g/4 oz /2 cups	fresh breadcrumbs
	Grated rind of 1¹⁄₂ lemons
60 g/2 oz/³⁄₄ cup	no-need-to-soak dried apricots, chopped
1	onion, finely chopped
60 g/2 oz /¹⁄₂ cup	walnuts, chopped
1 tablespoon	chopped sage
1 tablespoon	chopped parsley
175 g/6 oz /1 cup	cooked ham, chopped
1	egg, beaten
	Salt and pepper
250 ml/8 fl oz /1 cup	mayonnaise
125 ml/4 fl oz /¹⁄₂ cup	fromage frais
1 tablespoon	lemon juice

Slice the chicken breasts in half horizontally. Butter a large piece of greaseproof (wax) paper. Mix the breadcrumbs, two-thirds of the lemon rind, the apricots, onion, walnuts, herbs, ham and egg. Add plenty of seasoning and make sure the ingredients are thoroughly combined.

Arrange four slices of chicken in an oblong shape on the buttered paper. Press half the stuffing over the top. Cover with a further four slices of chicken and add the remaining stuffing. Lastly, lay the remaining slices of chicken over the top. Seal the ballotine firstly in the paper, then in a double-thick foil wrapping.

Place the ballotine in a large saucepan or deep roasting tin and pour in water to come two-thirds of the way up the package. Bring the water to the boil, then cover the pan and simmer the ballotine for 1¹⁄₂ hours. Top up the water, if necessary, with freshly boiling water from a kettle. Lift the ballotine from the water and leave to cool without unwrapping it. Chill for at least 2 hours.

Mix the remaining lemon rind with the mayonnaise, fromage frais, lemon juice and seasoning to taste. Use a serrated knife to slice the ballotine and serve the lemon mayonnaise as an accompaniment.

 **CHICKEN IN LEMON SAUCE**

SERVES 4

4	small boneless chicken breasts, skinned
1 teaspoon	sesame oil
4 tablespoons	dry sherry
	Juice of 1 lemon
6 tablespoons	cornflour (cornstarch)
1	egg, separated
	Grated rind of 2 lemons
2 teaspoons	sugar
	Salt and pepper
250 ml/8 fl oz /1 cup	chicken stock
3 tablespoons	sunflower oil
4	spring onions (scallions), finely shredded at an angle

Place the chicken breasts in a dish. Add the sesame oil, sherry and lemon juice. Cover and leave to marinate for at least 1 hour. Whisk the egg white lightly. Put 5 tablespoons of the cornflour in a dish. Drain the chicken, reserving the marinade, and dip each breast in egg white and coat with cornflour.

Prepare the sauce before cooking the chicken. Heat the reserved marinade with the lemon rind, sugar, seasoning and chicken stock. Mix the remaining cornflour with the egg yolk and 2 tablespoons water to make a smooth paste. Stir in the hot stock mixture. Pour the sauce back into the pan and bring to the boil, stirring all the time. Simmer for 3 minutes.

To cook the chicken, heat the oil in a large frying pan (skillet). Add the breasts and cook over medium heat until they are golden brown underneath. Turn the breasts over and cook until the second side is golden and the breasts are cooked through – this takes about 5 minutes on each side. Drain the cooked chicken on paper towels, then place the portions on a warmed serving platter and slice them. Separate the slices slightly. Spoon the sauce over the chicken and sprinkle with the spring onions. Serve at once.

NEXT PAGE: Zesty Chicken and Potato Curry (p.28); hard-boiled eggs with Lemon Curry Dressing (p.42); Lemon Pickle (p.38)

 # LIGHT MEALS

Here are a few ideas to revive your interest in the minor eating occasions. When you are trying to avoid nibbling between meals, remember that a glass of mineral water with a couple of slices of lemon makes a refreshing drink.

FATIMAS'S FINGERS

SERVES 4

125 g/4 oz	can sardines in oil
	Coarsely grated rind of 1 lemon
1	small garlic clove, crushed
$^1{}_2$	small onion, finely chopped
2 tablespoons	chopped parsley
$^1{}_2$ teaspoon	dried oregano
1 tablespoon	lemon juice
	Salt and pepper
4	large sheets filo pastry (about 45 x 20 cm/18 x 8 inches)
45 g/1$^1{}_2$ oz/3 tablespoons	butter, melted

Mash the sardines with the oil from the can, then mix in the lemon rind, garlic, onion, parsley, oregano, lemon juice and seasoning to taste.

Lay a sheet of filo on a clean, dry surface. Brush it lightly with melted butter and lay a second sheet on top. Use a sharp knife to cut the pastry in half lengthways. Then cut both pieces widthways into fingers measuring about 7.5 cm/3 inches wide. You should have 12 portions of pastry measuring 10 x 7.5 cm/4 x 3 inches.

Divide the filling roughly in half. Use one half to fill the 12 portions of pastry. Place a little filling at one end of each pastry finger. Brush a little butter around the edges of the pastry. Fold the sides over and roll up the filling in the pastry to make a small, neat finger. Brush the end of the pastry with a little melted butter, if necessary, to secure it. Prepare the remaining sheets of filo in the same way and fill with the remaining filling.

Lay the fingers on a baking sheets and brush them with a little melted butter. Bake at 190°C/375°F/gas 5 for 12-15 minutes, until golden brown and crisp. Cool on a wire rack. Serve hot, warm or cold.

 ## Flageolet Plaki

SERVES 4

Small, oval, pale green flageolet beans have a delicate flavour and pleasing bite to their texture. Prepare this gratin-style lunch dish in individual flameproof pots for the most attractive result. Small ramekin-dish portions also make a good first course for dinner.

Cook a chopped onion and a crushed garlic clove in a little butter until well softened but not browned. Stir in two drained 425 g/15 oz cans flageolet beans and a 400 g/14 oz can chopped tomatoes. Add seasoning and 1 teaspoon granulated sugar. Simmer for 10 minutes, then transfer to one large or four individual gratin dishes or pots to go under the grill (broiler).

Mix 90 g/3 oz/1½ cups fresh breadcrumbs with 2 tablespoons chopped parsley and the coarsely grated rind of 1 lemon. Sprinkle this topping over the bean mixture. Dot with butter and grill (broil) well away from the heat until crisp and golden.

ABOVE: Fatima's Fingers; Flageolet Plaki

 35

 **KIPPER CAKES**

These are quick and delicious! Canned kipper fillets
are a terrific standby to keep in reserve as they are
bone-free.

SERVES 4

1	onion, grated
175 g/6 oz/3 cups	fresh white breadcrumbs
	Grated rind of 1 lemon
4 tablespoons	chopped parsley
1 tablespoon	chopped tarragon
	Salt and pepper
190 g/6$\frac{1}{2}$ oz	can kipper fillets in oil
1	egg
	Juice of $\frac{1}{2}$ lemon
	Oil for cooking

Mix the onion, breadcrumbs, lemon rind, herbs and plenty of seasoning. Drain the oil from the kippers over the mixture. Flake the fish into the breadcrumb mixture. Stir the ingredients until well combined, then mix in the egg and lemon juice.

Shape the mixture into four or eight cakes. Heat a little oil in a frying pan (skillet) and cook the cakes over medium heat until golden brown on both sides. Serve with salad, new or baked potatoes.

 CHICK-PEA MAYONNAISE

SERVES 4

Chick-peas (garbanzo beans) and lentils are my favourite pulses for their versatility and flavour. I always keep canned chick-peas at the ready for whizzing up a stir-fry or making an interesting meal with minced (ground) meat or smoked sausage. This salad is one of my stand-by lunches – it's great with chunks of crusty bread or good in baked potatoes for a substantial snack.

Mix two drained 425 g/15 oz cans chick-peas with 4-6 chopped spring onions (scallions), 2 diced celery sticks, 1 crushed garlic clove, 4 tablespoons chopped parsley and the coarsely grated rind of 1 lemon. Stir 2 tablespoons tahini (sesame paste) and 2 tablespoons Greek yoghurt into 200 ml/7 fl oz/ $^3/_4$ cup mayonnaise and toss this with the chick-peas. Add a few sliced black olives if you like and pile the mixture on a bed of shredded salad leaves. Dust the top with a little paprika and garnish with lemon slices, whole olives and parsley.

ABOVE: Kipper Cakes (p.36)

PRESERVES & SAUCES

This chapter merely hints at the potential of lemons in preserves. Lemon peel, pith and pips (seeds) are rich in pectin and the juice is acidic – two vital attributes for setting jams, marmalades and jellies. Add the juice to less acidic fruit when making jams and use the whole fruit to make tangy marmalade. Lemon rind and juice may also be added to chutneys and pickles.

LEMON PICKLE

MAKES ABOUT 900 g/2 lb	
10	lemons, scrubbed and roughly chopped
12	garlic cloves, chopped
4 tablespoons	salt
5 tablespoons	granulated or preserving sugar
2 tablespoons	chilli powder
3 tablespoons	garam masala
900 g/2 lb	onions, chopped
300 ml/ ^{1}⁄2 pint/1 ^{1}⁄4 cups	oil
200 ml/7 fl oz/ ^{3}⁄4 cup	white vinegar

Discard the pips (seeds) from the lemons, then place the fruit in a bowl with the garlic, salt, sugar, chilli powder and garam masala. Mix well, cover and leave to stand for 48 hours, stirring occasionally.

Cook the onions in about a quarter of the oil for 10 minutes without allowing them to brown. Add the lemon mixture, the remaining oil and the vinegar. Bring to the boil, cover the pan and simmer for 1 hour, stirring often. Transfer to heated jars, cover at once with vinegar-proof lids and allow to mature for at least 2 weeks. Stir well before use. Serve this chilli-hot pickle with curries and spicy foods.

 ## FRESH DATE RELISH

This is a refreshing side dish for serving with
grilled lamb, chicken pork or gammon.

SERVES 4

Rub the skins off 125 g/4 oz fresh dates, slit them and remove their stones (pits), then slice them thinly. Finely chop
½ small onion and mix it with the dates. Pare the rind from ½ lemon, cut it into fine shreds and simmer these in water
for 5 minutes.

Meanwhile, roast 1 tablespoon crushed coriander seeds and 1 tablespoon pine kernels together in a dry pan until
the pine kernels are lightly browned. Add the drained lemon rind, 2 tablespoons olive oil and 2 tablespoons lemon
juice. Cook, stirring for 2 minutes, then pour this mixture over the dates. Mix well and leave to stand for 30 minutes.
Sprinkle a little freshly shredded mint over the relish before serving.

ABOVE: Fresh Date Relish on a cheeseboard

 **LEMON BAY SYRUP**

MAKES 600 ml/1 pint/2¹2 cups   Aromatic bay leaves and fragrant lemons make an
exotic dessert syrup. Spoon it over pancakes,
waffles, fresh fruit or ice-cream. Use it to moisten
and flavour plain cakes before filling with whipped
cream. Trickle it over a savarin or a sponge cake
base for a trifle.

Roughly chop a large lemon, discarding the pips (seeds), and place it in a saucepan. Add 6 bay leaves, 4 cloves and
1.15 litres/2 pints/5 cups water. Bring to the boil, reduce the heat and cover the pan. Simmer for 1 hour, leave to cool.
    Strain the liquid. Return it to the pan and add 350 g/12 oz/1¹2 cups granulated sugar. Bring the syrup to the boil,
stirring until the sugar has dissolved. Boil the syrup, uncovered, until reduced by half – about 15 minutes. Leave to
cool. Store in an airtight jar in the refrigerator for 2-3 months or freeze if making in large batches for longer storage.

 ## LEMON PINEAPPLE PRESERVE

MAKES about 1.75 kg/4 lb

Chop 4 large lemons roughly. Place them in a saucepan, adding the pips (seeds), with 2.25 litres/4 pints/2$\frac{1}{2}$ quarts water and 1 cinnamon stick. Bring to the boil, reduce the heat and cover the pan. Simmer for 2 hours, or until the lemons are tender. Place the fruit in a fine nylon sieve (strainer) and press all the liquid out of it. Discard the pulp that remains. Add two 375 g/13 oz cans crushed pineapple in juice and 900 g/2 lb/4 cups granulated or preserving sugar. Stir until the sugar has dissolved, then bring to the boil and boil hard until the preserve reaches setting point.

Test for setting using a sugar thermometer: when the fruit boils at 104°C/220°F, the sugar concentration is right for setting. You may also try a saucer test by putting a little of the preserve on a cold saucer. It should form a skin which wrinkles when pushed. Pot the preserve in hot sterilized jars. Cover immediately with waxed paper and airtight lids.

ABOVE: LEFT TO RIGHT: Lemon Pineapple Preserve; Lemon Bay Syrup

Sauces, Dressings & Butters

Anchovy Butter

Mash a 50 g/2 oz can anchovies thoroughly with the oil from the can. Mix with the grated rind of 1 lemon, 1 tablespoon lemon juice and 125 g/4 oz/ $\frac{1}{2}$ cup butter. Add pepper. Serve with grilled (broiled) fish or steaks; use instead of garlic butter to make a savoury bread or serve on toast.

Lemon Apple Sauce

Peel, core and slice 450 g/1 lb cooking apples. Place in a saucepan with the pared and finely shredded rind of 1 lemon and the juice from the fruit. Add 125 g/4 oz/ $\frac{1}{2}$ cup granulated sugar (or to taste) and heat until it has melted. Then bring to simmering point, cover the pan and cook, stirring occasionally, for 30 minutes, until the apples are pulpy and the rind tender. Beat in a knob of unsalted butter to enrich the sauce. Serve hot or cold with roast pork or grilled gammon, or with desserts, such as pancakes, waffles or plain sponge pudding.

Lemon Caramel

Grate the rind from a large lemon. Place 225 g/8 oz/ 1 cup granulated sugar, 125 ml/4 fl oz/ $\frac{1}{2}$ cup water and the juice from the lemon in a saucepan. Heat, stirring, until the sugar has dissolved, then bring to the boil. Boil until the syrup turns a deep golden colour without stirring. Remove the pan from the heat and immerse its base in a bowl or sink of cold water to prevent further cooking. Add the lemon rind to the caramel and stir in 2 tablespoons boiling water. Do this carefully, keeping the pan at arm's length as it spits dangerously. Cool, then store in an airtight jar in the refrigerator where it will keep for several months.

Lemon Curry Dressing

Cook 1 small, finely chopped onion in 2 tablespoons oil until soft but not browned. Add 1 tablespoon good curry powder and the grated rind of 1 lemon. Cook for 2 minutes, then stir in 1 tablespoon lemon juice and 2 tablespoons mango chutney, first chopping any large pieces of fruit. Cool. Mix with 300 ml/ $\frac{1}{2}$ pint/1 $\frac{1}{4}$ cups mayonnaise or fromage frais. Use to dress cooked chicken, turkey or prawns (shrimp).

SAUCES, DRESSINGS & BUTTERS

LEMON MAYONNAISE

Add the grated rind of 1 lemon and 2 tablespoons lemon juice to 300 ml/ ½ pint/1¼ cups good mayonnaise. Stir in 2 tablespoons snipped chives or parsley, if liked.

LEMON SAUCE FOR FISH OR CHICKEN

Cook 1 bay leaf and 1 chopped onion in 60 g/2 oz/ ¼ cup butter until soft but not browned. Stir in the grated rind of 1 lemon and 30 g/1 oz/2 tablespoons plain (all-purpose) flour. Add 475 ml/16 fl oz/2 cups fish or chicken stock gradually and bring to the boil, stirring. Simmer for 5 minutes. Beat 2 egg yolks with a little of the sauce and 3 tablespoon single (light) cream. Off the heat, stir the egg mixture into the sauce. Heat gently for a few seconds without simmering. Add a little chopped parsley and taste for seasoning.

MAITRE D'HOTEL BUTTER

Cream the grated rind of 1 lemon with 125 g/4 oz/ ½ cup butter. Work in 4 tablespoons finely chopped parsley and 1 tablespoon lemon juice. Form into a roll in a piece of cling film (plastic wrap) and chill until firm. Slice and serve on grilled fish, steaks or chops.

SWEET LEMON BUTTER

Cream 125 g/4 oz/ ½ cup unsalted butter with 60 g/2 oz/ ⅓ cup icing (confectioners') sugar and the grated rind of 1 lemon. Beat in the juice of ½ lemon gradually. Good with pancakes, waffles and fritters.

SWEET LEMON SAUCE

Mix 90 g/3 oz/ ⅓ cup granulated sugar, 30 g/1 oz/ ¼ cup cornflour (cornstarch) and the grated rind and juice of 2 lemons to a smooth paste. Add water to make 475 ml/16 fl oz/2 cups. Bring to the boil, whisking all the time, then simmer for 5 minutes. Beat 2 egg yolks with 125 ml/4 fl oz/ ½ cup double (heavy) cream. Remove the sauce from the heat and stir in the cream. Serve hot with sponge pudding or fruit pie.

 # DESSERTS

Many popular desserts rely on lemons for success, from steaming hot puddings to iced delights. This chapter offers a selection of favourite recipes with a twist of citrus.

CITRUS DELIGHT

SERVES 4

4	small slices plain cake or individual cakes, such as plain cup cakes
175 g/6 oz	raspberries or mixed soft fruit
4 tablespoons	orange liqueur, such as Cointreau or Curaçao
2	egg yolks
2 tablespoons	cornflour (cornstarch)
	Grated rind and juice of 2 lemons
4 tablespoons	caster (superfine) sugar
125 ml/4 fl oz/^{1}2 cup	medium sherry
250 ml/8 fl oz/1 cup	single (light) cream
125 ml/4 fl oz/^{1}2 cup	milk
150 ml/ 1/4 pint/^{2}3 cup	double (heavy) cream

Crumble the pieces of cake into individual dishes. Reserve four of the raspberries for decoration, then divide the remainder between the dishes. Sprinkle the orange liqueur over the fruit and set aside.

Whisk the egg yolks with the cornflour, lemon rind and juice, sugar and sherry until smooth. Stir in the single cream and pour the mixture into a small saucepan. Bring to the boil, whisking lightly all the time. When the mixture has thickened, whisk in the milk slowly and simmer gently for 2 minutes. Cool the lemon mixture slightly before pouring it over the raspberries. Cover the surface of the custard with dampened greaseproof (waxed) paper or cling film (plastic wrap) and leave until cold. Then chill the desserts for several hours or overnight.

Whip the double cream until it stands in soft peaks and pipe swirls on the desserts. Decorate with the reserved raspberries just before serving.

Exotic Ice

SERVES 6

	Grated rind and juice of 3 lemons
90 g/3 oz/⅓ cup	granulated sugar
475 ml/16 fl oz/2 cups	mango or pineapple juice
125 ml/4 fl oz/½ cup	water
125 g/4 oz/1 cup	chopped candied ginger
DECORATION:	
1	mango, peeled and sliced
1	lemon, sliced

Place the lemon rind and juice, sugar, mango or pineapple juice and water in a saucepan. Heat, stirring, until the sugar has dissolved, then bring to the boil. Boil for 5 minutes. Set aside to cool.

Pour the cold syrup into a freezer container. Freeze until the edges of the syrup form ice – about 3 hours. Process the mixture in a food processor or use an electric beater to whisk it thoroughly until smooth. Repeat this freezing and whisking twice more. By this time the syrup should form a thick, smooth ice sludge. Stir in the ginger and freeze until firm.

Allow to stand in the refrigerator for 15-20 minutes, until the ice is soft enough to scoop. Serve decorated with slices of fresh mango and lemon.

Summer Charlotte

SERVES 8

	Pared rind and juice of 4 lemons
60 g/2 oz/¼ cup	granulated sugar
3 teaspoons	gelatine
250 g/8 oz	raspberries
250 g/8 oz	strawberries, sliced
18 cm/7 inch	round sponge cake
250 ml/8 fl oz/1 cup	double (heavy) cream
	Whole strawberries for decoration

Place the lemon rind in a saucepan with water to cover. Bring to the boil, reduce the heat and cover the pan. Simmer for 30 minutes, then leave to cool slightly. Strain the liquid and add the lemon juice. Make the liquid up to 750 ml/ 1¼ pints/3 cups with hot water. Stir in the sugar until it has dissolved, then sprinkle the gelatine over and stir until that has dissolved too. Spoon a little of the lemon jelly into the base of an 18 cm/7 inch deep round cake tin to form a thin layer and chill it in the freezer briefly until set. Arrange a few raspberries and strawberry slices on the layer of jelly, spoon in some more jelly and chill in the freezer briefly until set.

Slice the sponge cake horizontally so that you have four layers. Layer the cake and remaining fruit in the tin, then pour in the jelly and chill overnight until set. To unmould the charlotte, dip the tin quickly in hot water, cover it with a flat platter and invert both platter and mould. Remove the mould. Whip the cream and pipe swirls around the base of the charlotte. Decorate with whole strawberries. Serve with the remaining whipped cream.

NEXT PAGE: LEFT TO RIGHT: Alaska Surprise (p.46); Citrus Delight; Exotic Ice

 ## Alaska Surprise

Serves 8

90 g/3 oz/6 tablespoons	butter, softened
175 g/6 oz/³⁄₄ cup	caster (superfine) sugar
	Grated rind of 2 lemons
1	egg plus 2 whites
90 g/3 oz/³⁄₄ cup	self-raising (rising) flour
	Juice of ¹⁄₂ lemon
250 g/8 oz/1 cup	lemon curd (see below)
1 litre/1³⁄₄ pints/1 quart	good-quality vanilla ice-cream (not soft scoop)
30 g/1 oz/¹⁄₄ cup	flaked (slivered) almonds

Cream the butter and half the sugar until pale and light. Beat in the rind of 1 lemon and the whole egg, adding a small spoonful of the flour. Use a metal spoon to fold in the remaining flour, then the lemon juice. Spread the mixture in a well-greased 20cm(8 inch) sponge flan tin (pie plate) and bake at 180°C/350°F/gas 4 for about 20-25 minutes, until risen, golden and springy to the touch. Turn out and cool on a wire rack.

At least 2 hours before serving spread the lemon curd in the sponge flan, fill it with ice-cream and place in the freezer for 2 hours before serving. Whisk the egg whites until stiff. Whisk in the remaining sugar gradually, and continue whisking until the meringue mixture is very glossy. Fold in the remaining lemon rind. Place the flan on a baking sheet. Cover it completely with the meringue mixture, sprinkle with the almonds and cook at 240°C/475°F/gas 9 for about 3 minutes, until tinged brown, and serve at once.

Home-Made Lemon Curd

Makes about 900 g/2 lb
Beat 2 egg yolks with the grated rind and juice of 2 lemons and 250 g/8 oz/1 cup caster (superfine) sugar in a heatproof bowl. Stand the bowl over a saucepan of barely simmering water – do not allow it to boil or the curd will curdle. Add 90 g/3 oz/6 tablespoons unsalted butter, cut in small pieces. Stir the mixture continuously until the butter has melted and the curd has thickened enough to coat the back of a spoon lightly. This takes about 20 minutes. Do not overcook or overheat the curd or the eggs will curdle. Place in thoroughly hot, sterilized jars and cover at once with waxed discs. Leave to cool before putting lids on the pots. Store in the refrigerator and use within 3-4 weeks.

CITRUS CREPES

SERVES 4

60 g/2 oz/ ^{1}₃ cup	sultanas (golden raisins)
1	lemon
125 g/4 oz/1 cup	plain (all-purpose) flour
2	eggs
300 ml/ ^{1}₂ pint/1 ^{1}₄ cups	milk
1 tablespoon	oil
1 tablespoon	water
	Butter for cooking
3 tablespoons	icing (confectioners') sugar
225 g/8 oz/1 cup	cream cheese
30 g/1 oz/2 tablespoons	granulated sugar
60 g/2 oz/ ^{1}₄ cup	unsalted butter
4 tablespoons	medium sherry

Place the sultanas in a small bowl. Pare the rind from the lemon, then shred it finely and simmer it in water to cover for 10 minutes. Drain, reserve the water, and set aside. Meanwhile, squeeze the lemon and pour the juice over the sultanas. Cover and set aside.

Place the flour in a bowl. Make a well in the middle and add the eggs with a little of the milk. Beat the eggs and a little of the milk into the flour, adding more milk gradually to make a smooth batter. Beat in the oil and water. Use this batter to make 12 pancakes, cooking them in a butter-greased pan. Layer paper towels between the pancakes, then wrap them in foil and keep warm.

Mix the sultanas and lemon juice, icing sugar and cream cheese. Measure 125 ml/4 fl oz/ ^{1}₂ cup of the reserved water from cooking the lemon rind. Bring it to the boil with the sugar and unsalted butter, stirring, then boil hard for 3 minutes, until slightly reduced. Remove from the heat and stir in the lemon rind and sherry. Spread the cheese mixture over the pancakes and fold each in four. Serve on warmed plates, with the lemon sherry syrup trickled over.

 ## SPECIAL BREAD PUDDING

Cooked pared lemon rind adds a zesty flavour to a rich version of a traditional family pudding. Lightly sweetened strawberry purée makes a summery sauce to serve with the pudding – and it is an ideal way of using frozen fruit during winter months.

SERVES 6

	Pared rind of 2 lemons
90 g/3 oz/6 tablespoons	unsalted butter
6	slices white bread, crusts removed
4 tablespoons	clear honey
	A little grated nutmeg
60 g/2 oz/ ¹3 cup	sultanas (golden raisins)
3	eggs, beaten
475 ml/16 fl oz/2 cups	milk
250 ml/8 fl oz/1 cup	single (light) cream
30 g/1 oz/ ¹4 cup	flaked (slivered) almonds
1-2 tablespoons	icing (confectioners') sugar
350 ml/12 fl oz/1¹2 cups	strawberry purée

Cut the lemon rind into fine shreds, cook them in boiling water for 15 minutes and drain. Grease an ovenproof dish with a little of the butter.

Spread the remaining butter on the bread, then spread each slice thickly with honey and sprinkle with a little nutmeg. Cut the bread slices into quarters and arrange them in the dish. Sprinkle each layer of bread with lemon rind and sultanas. Beat the eggs with the milk and stir in the cream. Strain the mixture over the bread and set aside to soak for 15 minutes.

Sprinkle the almonds over the pudding and bake at 180°C/350°F/gas 4 for 40 minutes, until the custard mixture has set and the almonds are lightly browned. Stir the icing sugar into the strawberry purée to sweeten it lightly to taste. Serve the pudding hot or warm, and offer the strawberry purée separately.

 **LEMON BOODLE**

SERVES 4

The name Boodle is usually given to an orange cream which originates from the menu at Boodles club in London. This is a quick lemon cream, served on a cake base.

Cut 4 slices off a plain Madeira cake. Break up the slices into four glass dishes, keeping the cake in chunks rather than crumbs. Sprinkle a little medium sherry over each portion. Grate the rind and squeeze the juice of 2 lemons, whisk in 4 tablespoons icing (confectioners') sugar and add 300 ml/ ¹⁄₂ pint/1¹⁄₄ cups double (heavy) cream. Whip the cream until it stands in soft peaks. Taste for sweetness before dividing the mixture between the glasses, spooning it over the cake. Chill for 1-2 hours before serving. Meanwhile cook fine shreds of pared lemon rind in simmering water for 15 minutes and drain them well. Sprinkle the shreds over the boodle before serving.

ABOVE: TOP: Lemon Boodle - BOTTOM: Special Bread Pudding

 **BAKING**

Lemons take to breads, cakes and biscuits with ease, adding a full, fresh flavour which contrasts well with the sweet base mixture. Try the recipes in this chapter to discover the tang of citrus baking, both sweet and savoury.

LEMON SHORTBREAD

MAKES 14 fingers	175 g/6 oz/³4 cup	unsalted butter
	60 g/2 oz/¹4 cup	caster (superfine) sugar
	2 tablespoons	icing (confectioners') sugar
		Grated rind of 2 lemons
	250 g/9 oz/2¹4 cups	plain (all-purpose) flour

Cream the butter with both types of sugar until thoroughly softened and creamy. Beat in the lemon rind, then mix in the flour to make a soft dough. Knead the dough very lightly on a floured surface, then press it into a greased 17.5 cm/7 inch square shallow baking tin. Prick the dough all over and chill it for at least 30 minutes.

Bake the shortbread at 160°C/325°F/gas 3 for 50-60 minutes, until pale gold. While the shortbread is still hot from the oven, use a serrated knife to cut it into 2.5 cm/1 inch wide fingers. Leave to cool in the tin for about 3 minutes. Carefully remove one finger – this will probably be a reject and you will have to eat it straightaway – then the remaining shortbread fingers will come out more easily. Cool the shortbread on a wire rack.

TOPPING IDEAS Before chilling, you may like to sprinkle a topping over the shortbread. Chopped walnuts, flaked almonds, finely chopped candied peel, chopped candied or crystallized ginger are all suitable. Whole nuts and halved glacé (candied) cherries may also be arranged on the shortbread.

 **GOUGÈRES**

The basic gougère is a small cheese-flavoured choux pastry bun or ring which is traditionally served cold at wine tastings. It is an excellent accompaniment for soups or starters. It may be filled with a savoury mixture or salad and served hot or cold.

MAKES 12

125 ml/4 fl oz/ ^{1}2 cup	water
60 g/2 oz/ ^{1}4 cup	butter
	Grated rind of 1 lemon
65 g/2^{1}2 oz/generous ^{1}2 cup	plain (all-purpose) flour
	Pinch of salt
2	eggs
125 g/4 oz/1 cup	Gruyère cheese, grated
2 tablespoons	chopped parsley
3 tablespoons	snipped chives

Place the water, butter and lemon rind in a saucepan. Heat gently until the butter melts, then bring the mixture to the boil as quickly as possible. Immediately the liquid boils, tip in all the flour, remove the pan from the heat and stir until the mixture forms a ball of paste which leaves the sides of the pan clean. Do not beat the paste: set it aside to cool for 10 minutes.

Beat the eggs into the paste and continue beating until it is very smooth and glossy. Beat in three-quarters of the cheese, the parsley and chives. Spoon the mixture into a piping bag fitted with a large plain tube (tip). Pipe rings of mixture on two greased baking sheets. Sprinkle the remaining cheese over the choux rings and bake at 220°C/425°F/gas 7 for 15 minutes. Reduce the oven temperature to 190°C/375°F/gas 5 and cook for a further 10-15 minutes, until the gougères are golden and crisp. Make a split in each gougère to allow the steam to escape, then cool them on a wire rack. Serve either warm or cold.

 **LEMON DATE BAKEWELL**

SERVES 8

	Grated rind and juice of 2 lemons
60 g/2 oz/ ^{1}⁄3 cup	chopped candied peel
250 g/8 oz/1^1⁄2 cup	cooking dates, chopped
60 g/2 oz/ ^{1}⁄3 cup	glacé (candied) cherries, chopped
30 g/1 oz/3 tablespoons	soft brown sugar
175 g/6 oz/1^1⁄2 cups	plain (all-purpose) flour
175 g/6 oz/ ^{3}⁄4 cup	butter or margarine
90 g/3 oz/6 tablespoons	caster (superfine) sugar
1-2 tablespoons	water
1	egg
60 g/2 oz/ ^{1}⁄2 cup	self-raising (rising) flour
30 g/1 oz/ ^{1}⁄4 cup	ground almonds
^{1}⁄2 teaspoon	natural almond essence (extract)
30 g/1 oz/ ^{1}⁄4 cup	flaked (slivered) almonds
4 tablespoons	orange jelly marmalade, warmed and sieved (optional)
	Icing (confectioners') sugar to dust (optional)

Place the rind and juice of 1 lemon, the candied peel, dates, cherries and soft brown sugar in a small saucepan. Heat stirring, until the sugar melts, then remove from the heat and set aside.

Place the flour in a bowl and rub in 125 g/4 oz/ ^{1}⁄2 cup of the butter or margarine. Stir in 2 tablespoons of the sugar and enough of the water to bind the mixture into a rich pastry dough. Roll out and use to line a 20 cm/8 inch flan tin (pie pan). Prick the pastry, then chill it for at least 30 minutes. Line the pastry with greaseproof (waxed) paper, sprinkle with baking beans and bake at 200°C/400°F/gas 6 for 35-40 minutes. Remove the paper and beans. Reduce the oven temperature to 180°C/350°F/gas 4.

Cream the remaining butter or margarine and caster sugar with the lemon rind until pale and soft. Beat in the egg, then fold in the flour, ground almonds, almond essence and lemon juice. Spread the date mixture over the base of the pastry, then top with the creamed mixture, spreading it as evenly as possible. Sprinkle with the flaked almonds and bake for about 30 minutes, until golden, set and springy to the touch. The flan may be glazed with orange jelly marmalade when warm and then dusted with icing sugar when cold, if liked. Serve warm or cold.

OPPOSITE: LEFT: Lemon Date Bakewell - RIGHT: Lemon Gingerbread

 **LEMON GINGERBREAD**

MAKES a 900 g/2 lb loaf cake	90 g/3 oz/6 tablespoons	butter
	90 g/3 oz/ 1⁄2 cup	soft brown sugar
	90 g/3 oz/6 tablespoons	golden (light corn) syrup
		Grated rind of 2 lemons
		Juice of 1 lemon
	125 g/4 oz/ 2⁄3 cup	chopped candied peel
	125 g/4 oz/1 1⁄4 cup	chopped glacé (candied) ginger
	250 g/8 oz/2 cups	plain (all-purpose) flour
	1 tablespoon	ground ginger
	1 teaspoon	bicarbonate of soda (baking soda)
	1	egg, beaten

Base-line and grease a 900 g/2 lb loaf tin. Heat the butter, sugar, syrup, lemon rind and juice, candied peel and glacé ginger gently, stirring occasionally, until the butter has melted and all the ingredients are thoroughly combined.

Sift the flour, ground ginger and bicarbonate of soda into a bowl. Make a well in the centre and add the egg, then pour in the melted mixture. Beat the ingredients together until thoroughly combined and turn the mixture into the prepared tin. Bake 160°C/325°F/gas 3 for 1 1⁄4-1 1⁄2 hours, until risen, golden and firm to the touch. Leave the gingerbread to cool in the tin for 30 minutes, then transfer it to a wire rack to cool completely.

Bombe Gateau

Serves 8	*3*	eggs
	90 g/3 oz/6 tablespoons	caster (superfine) sugar
		Grated rind and juice of 1 lemon
	90 g/3 oz/$\frac{3}{4}$ cup	plain (all-purpose) flour
Filling & Decoration	*300 ml/$\frac{1}{2}$ pint /$1\frac{1}{4}$ cups*	double (heavy) cream
	225 g/8 oz/1 cup	Lemon Curd (page 48)
	350 g/12 oz/3 cups	raspberries
		Chocolate curls (optional)
		Frosted leaves (see note)

Grease a 1.15 litre/2 pint/5 cup ovenproof pudding basin and stand it on a baking sheet. Whisk the eggs, sugar and lemon rind together until pale and very thick: the best way of doing this is over a pan of barely simmering water. Turn the mixture into the prepared basin and bake at 180°C/350°F/gas 4 for 45-50 minutes. Cool the cake on a wire rack.

Whip the cream until it stands in soft but fairly firm peaks. Fold in the lemon curd carefully. Use a serrated knife to slice the cake horizontally into four layers. Reserve about a quarter of the raspberries for the decoration. Sandwich the cake back together with layers of lemon cream and raspberries. Place some of the remaining cream in a piping bag fitted with a large star tube (tip). Cover the gâteau completely with cream and place it on a serving platter.

Pipe swirls around the base and in a ring around the top of the gâteau. Decorate with the reserved raspberries and chocolate curls if liked. A few frosted mint leaves may be added for a fresh colour.

Note   Select perfect, fresh leaves for frosting. Mint leaves are ideal. Brush them with a little lightly whisked egg white and sprinkle them with caster sugar. Set aside to dry.

 ## SAVOURY ANCHOVY TWISTS

MAKES about 24

225 g/8 oz/2 cups	plain (all-purpose) flour
125 g/4 oz/¹₂ cup	butter
	Grated rind of 2 lemons
50 g/2 oz	can anchovies, drained and finely chopped
2 tablespoons	very finely chopped onion
60 g/2 oz/¹₂ cup	mature Cheddar cheese, finely grated
About 2 tablespoons	water

Place the flour in a bowl and rub in the butter. Mix in the lemon rind, anchovies, onion and cheese. Add just enough water to bind the dough. Roll out the dough into a 30 x 23 cm/12 x 9 inch rectangle and cut into 24 strips measuring 23 x 1.25 cm/9 x ¹₂ inch. Twist each strip as you lay it on a baking sheet. Chill the twists for 30 minutes. Bake at 200°C/400°F/gas 6 for 20 minutes, until browned and cooked. Cool on a wire rack.

LEMON SNAPS

MAKES about 24

90 g/3 oz/6 tablespoons	butter
	Grated rind and juice of 1 lemon
6 tablespoons	golden (light corn) syrup
2 teaspoons	natural vanilla essence (extract)
¹₄ teaspoon	bicarbonate of soda (baking soda)
125 g/4 oz/1 cup	plain (all-purpose) flour

Grease two baking sheets or line them with non-stick baking parchment. Heat the butter, lemon rind and juice, golden syrup and vanilla together, stirring occasionally, until thoroughly combined. Cool slightly, then beat in the bicarbonate of soda and flour.

Drop medium-sized (dessertspoon) spoonfuls of mixture well apart on the baking sheets. Bake at 160°C/325°F/gas 3 for 20 minutes, until the biscuits are golden. Leave to cool on the baking sheets for about a minute, until the mixture has firmed slightly. Then transfer the biscuits to a wire rack to cool completely.

NEXT PAGE: CLOCKWISE: Lemon Snaps; Lemon Florentines (p.60); Lemon Ring Bread (p.61)

 ## LEMON FLORENTINES

MAKES about 12

	Grated rind and juice of 1 lemon
3 tablespoons	golden (light corn) syrup
45 g/1½ oz/3 tablespoons	butter
45 g/1½ oz/3 tablespoons	granulated sugar
60 g/2 oz/½ cup	plain (all-purpose) flour
2 tablespoons	finely chopped candied peel
2 tablespoons	chopped toasted hazelnuts
2 tablespoons	chopped angelica
2 tablespoons	chopped glacé cherries
125 g/4 oz/4 squares	white chocolate

Grease two baking sheets. Heat the lemon rind and juice, golden syrup, butter and sugar in a small saucepan, stirring occasionally, until the ingredients are thoroughly combined. Remove from the heat and mix in the flour, candied peel, hazelnuts, angelica and cherries.

Drop small spoonfuls of the mixture well apart on the greased baking sheets—you will probably only be able to cook four biscuits (cookies) to each sheet. Bake the biscuits, one baking sheet at a time, at 190°C/375°F/gas 5 for 5-8 minutes. Leave the biscuits to cool for about 30 seconds, or until the mixture is just firm enough to stay in shape when a knife is slid underneath it. Transfer the biscuits to a wire rack to cool. If the mixture hardens before you remove the biscuits from the baking sheets, then replace them in the oven for about 30 seconds to soften.

When the biscuits are cold, melt the chocolate in a basin over a pan of hot, not boiling, water. Coat the smooth side of each florentine with chocolate and use a fork to mark a pattern of wavy lines in the coating. Leave to set. Store in an airtight container.

 ## LEMON RING BREAD

This is ideal for Easter, when it may be decorated
with chocolate eggs instead of the flaked almonds.

MAKES a 23 cm/9 inch ring	450 g/1 lb/4 cups	strong plain (bread) flour
	1 teaspoon	salt
	90 g/3 oz/6 tablespoons	butter
	1 sachet	easy-blend yeast
	4 tablespoons	caster (superfine) sugar
		Grated rind of 2 lemons
	60 g/2 oz/ ^{1}3 cup	chopped candied peel
	125 g/4 oz/1 cup	blanched almonds, toasted and chopped
	60 g/2 oz/ ^{1}3 cup	white chocolate chips or cooking dots
	1 tablespoon	natural vanilla essence (extract)
	250 ml/8 fl oz/1 cup	hand-hot milk
		Beaten egg to glaze
	125 g/4 oz/ ^{2}3 cup	icing (confectioners') sugar
		Juice of 1 lemon
	30 g/1 oz/ ^{1}4 cup	flaked (slivered) almonds, toasted
	1	piece candied lemon peel, shredded

Mix the flour and salt in a bowl. Rub in the butter, then stir in the yeast, sugar, grated lemon rind, candied peel, chopped almonds and chocolate chips. Mix the vanilla and milk into the dry ingredients to form a dough. Turn the dough out on a floured surface and knead it until it is elastic and smooth. Divide the dough in half. Roll each piece into a long thin sausage shape, about 70-75 cm/28-30 inches long. Twist these together and form them into a ring on a greased baking sheet. Cover with lightly oiled polythene or cling film (plastic wrap) and set aside to rise for several hours. This will take very much longer than for ordinary bread dough.

Brush the ring with beaten egg and bake at 200°C/400°F/gas 6 for 45-50 minutes, or until it is browned and cooked through. Check by tapping the base of the loaf, which should sound hollow. Cool the ring on a wire rack.

Mix the icing sugar with just enough lemon juice to make a smooth, thick glacé icing. Drizzle this from side to side over the ring. Immediately top the ring with the flaked almonds and candied peel.

 # Lemon Cheesecakes

These make a change from a large cheesecake – they are ideal as a teatime treat or you may like to decorate them with piped whipped cream and top each with a strawberry for serving as a dessert.

Makes 16

Rub 125 g/4 oz/ ½ cup butter into 175 g/6 oz/1½ cups plain (all-purpose) flour. Mix in 2 tablespoons caster (superfine) sugar and 60 g/2 oz/ ½ cup chopped toasted hazelnuts. Bind the dough with 1 egg yolk and 1 tablespoon natural vanilla essence (extract). Roll out and cut out rounds to line 16 patty tins (shallow muffin pans). Prick the pastry cases, chill for 30 minutes, then bake at 200°C/400°F/gas 6 for 10 minutes. Reduce the oven temperature to 180°C/350°F/gas 5. Mix the grated rind and juice of 1 lemon, 250 g/8 oz/1 cup cream cheese, 2 tablespoons self-raising flour, 2 tablespoons caster sugar and 1 egg yolk. Whisk the egg white until stiff and fold it into the mixture. Spoon the mixture into the pastry cases and bake for 25- 35 minutes. Cool on a wire rack, then dust with icing (confectioners') sugar.

ABOVE: Lemon Cheesecakes

INDEX